FIRST GRADE MATH

Table of Contents

Introduction

Mathematics skills are utilized in every aspect of an individual's life, whether a student or an adult. These skills, however, involve more than just the computation of numbers. Organization, investigation, logical reasoning, and communication are also basic skills associated with mathematics. Students must develop a solid foundation in basic mathematics skills in order to meet the challenges of learning. Once armed with these tools, they can face new situations with confidence in their ability to solve problems and to make decisions.

The *First Grade Math* program is offered to develop and strengthen mathematics skills. Each page provides practice in one specified skill. The worksheet can be used to assess students' understanding of the concept before or after the classroom lesson, or it can be used by students who might benefit from additional practice, either at home or school.

Organization

Ten units cover the basic mathematics skills taught in the first grade. Students begin with a review of counting to 10. They then focus on addition and subtraction facts to 10. Afterward, students proceed to develop an understanding of place value to 100. Then the book introduces facts to 18. Finally, students explore geometry, measurement, fractions, time, and money. Fun, thematic worksheet titles attract students' interest. One page at the end of each unit is devoted solely to word problems which show how the learned skill might be applied to a real-world situation. These problems also provide practice in using a variety of problem-solving strategies.

Special Features

Each worksheet serves as practice for only one basic mathematics skill. Students who may need additional practice could benefit from these pages. Each page in the *First Grade Math* book also ends with a word problem. These problems deal only with the skill students are practicing. These word problems also provide examples of how mathematics skills can be applied to the real world.

Use

This book is designed for independent use by students who have had instruction in the specific skills covered in the lessons. Copies of the worksheets can be given to individuals, pairs of students, or small groups for completion. The worksheets can also be given as homework for reviewing and reinforcing basic mathematics skills.

To begin, determine the implementation that fits your students' needs and your classroom structure. The following plan suggests a format for this implementation:

1. Explain the purpose of the worksheets to your class.
2. Review the mechanics of how you want students to work with the exercises.
3. Review the specific skill for the students who may not remember the process for successful completion of the computation.
4. Introduce students to the process and to the purpose of the activities.
5. Do a practice activity together.
6. Discuss how students can use the skill as they work and play.

Additional Notes

1. A letter to parents is included on page 4. Send it home with the students and encourage them to share it with their parents.
2. Have fun with the pages. Math should be an enjoyable adventure that helps students grow, not only in math but also in their confidence and their ability to face new and challenging experiences.

Dear Parent,

Mathematics skills are important tools that your child will use throughout his or her life. These skills encompass more than just the computation of numbers. They involve the ability of individuals to organize, investigate, reason, and communicate. Thus, your child must develop a strong foundation of basic mathematics skills in the elementary grades so that he or she can expand and build on these skills to help navigate through the life experiences.

During the year, your child will be learning and practicing many mathematics skills in class. Some of the skills include counting and writing numbers, adding and subtracting facts to 18, telling time to the half hour, and simple fractions. After exploring the concepts associated with these basic skills, your child will bring home worksheets, whether completed in class or to be completed at home, designed to further practice these skills. To help your child progress at a faster rate, please consider the following suggestions:

- Together, review the work your child brings home or completes at home. Discuss any errors, and encourage your child to correct them.
- Encourage your child to make up word problems that apply to newly learned skills.
- Guide your child to see why it is important to learn math by pointing out ways that math is used in everyday life.
- Play games and solve puzzles with your child that utilize math skills.

Thank you for your help. Your child and I appreciate your assistance and reinforcement in this learning process.

Cordially,

Name _____   Date _____

Solve.

1.   2
     + 0

2.   13
      − 7

3.   3
     + 4

4. 11
    − 6

5.   8
     + 5

6. 16
    − 9

7.   6
     + 6

8. 14
    − 7

9.   9
     + 2

10.   8
      + 7

11. 18
     − 9

12.   9
      + 5

13. 12
     − 4

14.   5
      + 5

15. 10
     − 1

16. 13
     − 6

17.   7
      + 7

18.   9
      + 8

19. 5 − 0 = _____   **20.** 3 + 4 = _____

21. 9 + 5 = _____   **22.** 14 − 8 = _____

23. 9 + 7 = _____   **24.** 9 − 2 = _____

25. 8 − 4 = _____   **26.** 7 + 6 = _____

Assessment: Algorithms
Math 1, SV 8045-6

Name _____ Date _____

•••• GOING PLACES TO SOLVE PROBLEMS ••••

Solve.

1. Mr. Ladd sees 7 buses.
Then he sees 3 more buses.
How many buses does he see?

_____ + _____ = _____ buses

2. A train has 10 cars.
2 cars are taken off.
How many cars are left?

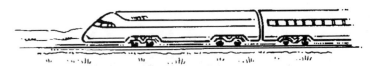

_____ – _____ = _____ cars

3. Mr. Carlos gets to work at 8 o'clock.
Write the time on the clock.

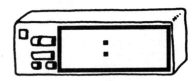

4. Inga saw 4 yield signs.
She saw 7 stop signs.
How many more stop signs did she
see?

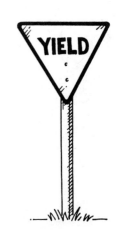

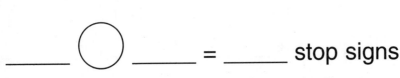

_____ ◯ _____ = _____ stop signs

Assessment: Word Problems

• • • • • • • • • • • • ANIMAL COUNT • • • • • • • • • • • • •

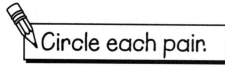 Circle each pair.

1.

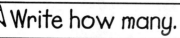 Write how many.

2.

2
_____

3.

_____

4.

_____

Real World Connection

Solve.

5. Tim went for a walk. He saw 3 squirrels.
Circle the group Tim saw.

Number Sense: Numbers to 3

© Steck-Vaughn Company

7

Math 1, SV 8045-6

Name _____ Date _____

•••••••• HEADS ABOVE THE REST ••••••••

 | Write how many. |

1.

5 _____

2.

_____

3.

_____

4.

_____

5.

_____

6.

_____

7.

_____

8.

_____

9.

_____

Real World Connection

Solve.

10. Circle the pictures that have the same number of clowns.

Number Sense: Numbers to 5

Math 1, SV 8045-6

TIGER TIME

Write how many. Circle the number word.

1.

6
_____

five   (six)

2.

_____

four   five

3.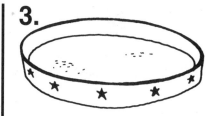

_____

zero   one

4.

_____

five   six

5.

_____

six   seven

6.

_____

two   three

Real World Connection

Solve.

7. The circus has these tigers. Lana saw six of them.
Circle the tigers that Lana saw.

Number Sense: Numbers to 7

Math 1, SV 8045-6

·········· A WALK IN THE PARK ··········

| Circle the groups that have 8.

1.

 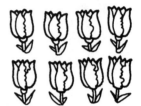

| Circle the groups that have 9.

2.

Real World Connection

Solve.

3. Kwan sees these frogs. Write how many frogs.

_____ frogs

Number Sense: Numbers to 9

10   Math 1, SV 8045-6

• • • • • • • • • • • AN OCEAN OF FUN • • • • • • • • • • •

Circle the number word. Then write the number.

1.

six
(nine)
ten

9

2.

five

six

seven

_____

3.

ten

three

two

_____

4.

eight

four

one

_____

Real World Connection

Solve.

5. Rita finds these shells.
Write how many shells.

_____ shells

Number Sense: Numbers to 10

Math 1, SV 8045-6

Name _____ Date _____

•••••••••• MONKEY BUSINESS ••••••••••

Write how many.

1.

3
_____

2.

_____

3.

_____

4.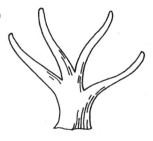

_____

5.

_____

6.

_____

Real World Connection

Solve.

7. There are five monkeys at the zoo.
Mr. Lee feeds a banana to each.
Circle the bowl he will use.

Number Sense: Zero

Math 1, SV 8045-6

Name _____ Date _____

•••••••• COUNTING IS JUST DUCKY! ••••••••

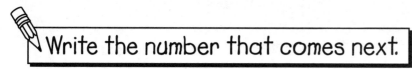

Write the number that comes next.

1.

3, 4, __5__

2.

8, 9, _____

3.

5, 6, _____

4.

0, 1, _____

5.

2, 3, _____

Count backward. Write the missing numbers.

6.

10, 9, ____ , ____ , ____ , 5, 4, ____ , 2, ____ , 0

7.

10, ____ , ____ , 7, 6, ____ , ____ , ____ , ____ , 1

Real World Connection

Solve.

8. Ben counts 6 ducks.
What will he count for the next duck?

_____

Number Sense: Order through 10

© Steck-Vaughn Company
Math 1, SV 8045-6

········ BUGGED ABOUT NUMBERS ········

Write how many. Then circle the number that is greater.

1.

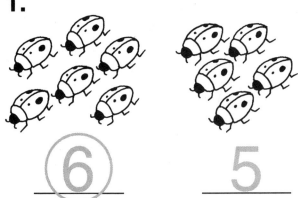

⑥   5
___   ___

2.

___   ___

Write how many. Then circle the number that is less.

3.

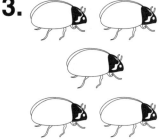

___   ___

4.

___   ___

Real World Connection

Solve.

5. Lee saw 8 bugs. Wes saw 0 bugs.
Who saw more bugs? _____

_____

Number Sense: Comparing Numbers

Name _____   Date _____

····· BUYING INTO PROBLEM SOLVING ·····

 Solve.

1. Marta buys these hats.
Write how many hats.

_____

2. Look at each purse.
Circle the purse that has more
pennies. Draw an X on the purse
that has fewer pennies.

3. Len buys these paints.
Write how many colors.

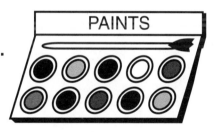

PAINTS

_____

4. Opal buys some cards.
Write the numbers of the
cards that she is missing.

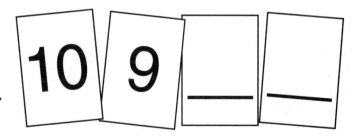

10 9 ___ ___

6 ___ ___ ___ 2 1

Number Sense: Word Problems

Math 1, SV 8045-6

•••••••••• JOIN IN THE FUN! ••••••••••

Write how many.

How many?	How many join?	How many in all?

1.       

4   1   5

____   ____   ____

2.       

____   ____   ____

3.       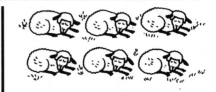

____   ____   ____

Real World Connection

Solve.

4. Jill has 4 hens. She gets 1 more hen.
Write how many hens in all.

_____

Addition to 10: Concept Development of Addition

    16   Math 1, SV 8045-6

·········· ANIMAL ADDING ··············

| Write the addition sentences and solve. |

1.

$$\underline{2} + \underline{1} = \underline{3}$$

2.

_____ + _____ = _____

3.

_____ + _____ = _____

4.

_____ + _____ = _____

5.

_____ + _____ = _____

Real World Connection

Solve.

6. Write an addition sentence and solve.

_____ + _____ = _____ dogs

17   **Addition to 10: Writing Addition Sentences**

Math 1, SV 8045-6

THE "WRITE" ORDER

Draw X to show how many. Write the sum.

1.
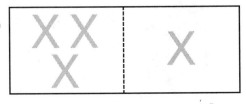 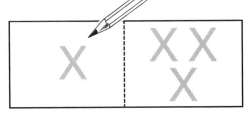

3 + 1 = __4__   1 + 3 = __4__

2.
 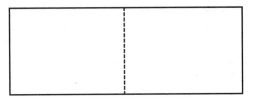

2 + 4 = _____   4 + 2 = _____

3.

3 + 2 = _____    2 + 3 = _____

Real World Connection

Solve.

4. Ray has these cubes.

Circle the pair that shows the same number.

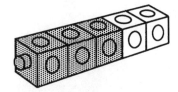 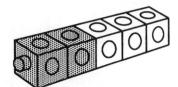 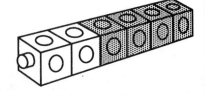

Addition to 10: Order in Addition

Math 1, SV 8045-6

• • • • • • • • • • • • • **NOTHING "HARE"** • • • • • • • • • • •

Draw dots to show how many. Write the sum.

1.

2 + 0 = _2_

2.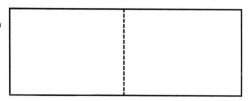

0 + 5 = _____

3.

1 + 0 = _____

4.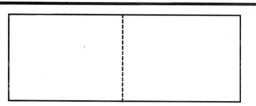

3 + 0 = _____

5.

0 + 4 = _____

Real World Connection

Solve.

6. Sally saw 6 rabbits in the grass.
She saw no rabbits by the garden.
How many rabbits did she see?

6 + 0 = _____ rabbits

Addition to 10: Adding 0
Math 1, SV 8045-6

······· LOOKING FOR "SUM" THING ·······

| Find ways to make the sums. |
| Then write the addition sentences. |

1. _____ + _____ = 3   **2.** _____ + _____ = 3

3. _____ + _____ = 3   **4.** _____ + _____ = 3

---

5. _____ + _____ = 4   **6.** _____ + _____ = 4

7. _____ + _____ = 4   **8.** _____ + _____ = 4

9. _____ + _____ = 4

---

10. _____ + _____ = 5   **11.** _____ + _____ = 5

12. _____ + _____ = 5   **13.** _____ + _____ = 5

14. _____ + _____ = 5   **15.** _____ + _____ = 5

Real World Connection

Write an addition sentence.

16. _____ + _____ = 5 socks

Addition to 10: Addition Combinations to 5

Math 1, SV 8045-6

···· THE UPS AND DOWNS OF ADDITION ····

Write the addition sentences and solve.

1.

_1_ + _3_ = _4_

$+ \begin{array}{r} 1 \\ 3 \\ \hline 4 \end{array}$

2.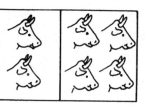

_____ + _____ = _____

$+ \rule{2cm}{0.4pt}$

3.

_____ + _____ = _____

$+ \rule{2cm}{0.4pt}$

Real World Connection

Write an addition sentence and solve.

4. 4 children are on the seesaw.

1 more boy comes to play.
How many children in all?

_____ + _____ = _____ children

$+ \rule{2cm}{0.4pt}$

Addition to 10: Vertical Addition

Math 1, SV 8045-6

• • • • • • • • • • • COUNTING ON A STAR • • • • • • • • • • •

Count on to add. Write each sum.

1.

| 4 | ★ |

4 + 1 = __5__

2.

| 4 | ★ ★ |

4 + 2 = _____

3.

| 8 | ★ |

8 + 1 = _____

4.

| 5 | ★ ★ |

5 + 2 = _____

5.

| 5 | ★ |

5 + 1 = _____

6.

| 2 | ★ ★ |

2 + 2 = _____

7. 6 + 1 = _____   **8.** 7 + 2 = _____   **9.** 8 + 2 = _____

Real World Connection

Write an addition sentence and solve.

10. Dan sees 6 stars. Dan sees 2 more stars.
How many stars does Dan see in all?

_____ + _____ = _____ stars

Addition to 10: Counting On

Math 1, SV 8045-6

Name _____   Date _____

Circle the greater number. Then add.

(7) (8)   2   (6) (7,8,9)
+ 1   +(6) (7,8)   + 3
___   ___   ___
8   8   9

---

1. 9   **2.** 6   **3.** 2   **4.** 4   **5.** 3
+ 1   + 2   + 3   + 2   + 4
___   ___   ___   ___   ___

---

6. 4   **7.** 2   **8.** 5   **9.** 1   **10.** 7
+ 1   + 8   + 3   + 4   + 3
___   ___   ___   ___   ___

Real World Connection

Write an addition sentence and solve.

11. 4 children play tug-of-war.

2 more children come to play.

How many children in all?

_____ + _____ = _____ children

Addition to 10: Counting on Using Mental Math

Name _____ Date _____

 · · · · · · · · · · · **DOUBLE THE MONEY** · · · · · · · · · · ·

| Complete each doubles fact. Write each sum. |

1. 4 + _4_ = _8_

2. 0 + _0_ = ___

---

3. 3
      + 3
     ____

4. 1
      + 1
     ____

5. 2
      + 2
     ____

6. 0
      + 0
     ____

7. 5
      + 5
     ____

| Write each sum. Circle each double. |

8. 2
      + 6
     ____

9. 7
      + 1
     ____

10. 3
       + 3
      ____

11. 6
       + 3
      ____

12. 5
       + 5
      ____

13. 4
       + 4
      ____

14. 3
       + 7
      ____

15. 2
       + 2
      ____

16. 2
       + 5
      ____

17. 1
       + 1
      ____

Real World Connection

Write an addition sentence and solve.

18. Jon has 3¢. Mary has double this amount.
How much money does Mary have?

_____ + _____ = _____ ¢

Addition to 10: Doubles

Name _____ Date _____

 Add.

1. $3 + 3 =$ ___6___

$3 + 4 =$ ___7___

2. $4 + 4 =$ _____

$4 + 5 =$ _____

---

3. 1
+ 1
___

4. 3
+ 2
___

5. 3
+ 7
___

6. 3
+ 3
___

7. 4
+ 3
___

8. 2
+ 3
___

9. 5
+ 5
___

10. 4
+ 4
___

11. 5
+ 4
___

12. 8
+ 2
___

Real World Connection

Write an addition sentence and solve.

13. Jose makes 5 points.
Russ makes 4 points.
How many points in all?

_____ + _____ = _____ points

Addition to 10: Doubles Plus 1

Math 1, SV 8045-6

Name _____   Date _____

Add. Start with the ringed numbers.

1. ③ + ③ + 4

___6___ + ___4___ = ___10___

2. ② + ⑤ + 1   **3.** 2 + ⑤ + ①

____ + ____ = ____   ____ + ____ = ____

Add.

4. 1	**5.** 4	**6.** 3	**7.** 6	**8.** 1
1	2	4	3	3
+ 8	+ 2	+ 1	+ 1	+ 5

9. 4	**10.** 1	**11.** 2	**12.** 3	**13.** 6
4	2	3	2	4
+ 1	+ 7	+ 4	+ 5	+ 0

Real World Connection

Write an addition sentence and solve.

14. Carol has 1 white marble,
5 striped marbles, and 4 spotted marbles.
How many marbles does she have in all?

____ + ____ + ____ = ____ marbles

Addition to 10: Adding 3 Numbers

26   Math 1, SV 8045-6

Name _____   Date _____

········ "SUM" THING ABOUT BIRDS ········

 Write the missing sums.

+	0	1	2	3	4	5	6	7	8
0	0	1	2		4	5		7	
1	1	2	3			6		8	9
2	2		4	5	6	7	8		10
3	3				7		9	10	
4	4	5	6		8	9			
5	5		7	8		10			
6	6	7		9					
7	7		9						
8	8		10						

Real World Connection

Solve.

Peter saw 3 red and 5 brown birds.
Jane saw 4 red and 4 brown birds.
Enrico saw 2 red and 7 brown birds.
Which children saw the same number of birds?

_____   _____

_ _ _ _ _ _ _ _ _ _   _ _ _ _ _ _ _ _ _ _

_____ and _____

Addition to 10: Addition Table
Math 1, SV 8045-6

········· **MOVING ALONG** ···············

 Add.

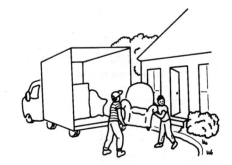

1. 3
  + 2

2. 5
  + 2

3. 1
  + 2

4. 2
  + 2

5. 5
  + 4

6. 8
  + 1

7. 1
  + 0

8. 7
  + 2

9. 3
  + 0

10. 7
  + 3

11. 5
  + 3

12. 4
  + 4

13. 6
  + 3

14. 7
  + 2

15. 5
  + 4

16. 9
  + 1

17. 8
  + 2

18. 6
  + 2

19. 4
  + 3

20. 4
  + 2

21. 8
  + 1

22. 5
  + 2

23. 5
  + 5

Real World Connection

Write an addition sentence and solve.

24. Sue moves 3 chairs.
Lan moves 5 chairs.
How many chairs do they move in all?

_____ + _____ = _____ chairs

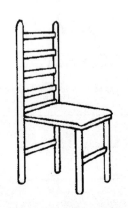

Addition to 10: Addition Practice

     Math 1, SV 8045-6

········ PRACTICE MAKES PERFECT ········

 Add.

1. 6
  + 2

2. 3
  + 6

3. 3
  + 3

4. 1
  + 9

5. 6
  + 0

6. 2
  + 8

7. 3
  + 5

8. 5
  + 2

9. 6
  + 1

10. 7
  + 3

11. 1
  + 7

12. 2
  + 2

13. 2
  + 3

14. 0
  + 0

15. 2
  + 4

16. 4
  + 3

17. 1
  + 6

18. 5
  + 5

19. 6
  + 4

20. 5
  + 3

21. 2
  + 6

22. 4
  + 4

23. 9
  + 0

Real World Connection

Write an addition sentence and solve.

24. Gail plays the piano for 2 hours on Saturday.
She plays for 3 hours on Sunday.
How many hours does she play in all?

_____ + _____ = _____ hours

Name _____   Date _____

····· PROBLEM SOLVING ON THE ROAD ·····

Write the addition sentences and solve.

1. There are 4 cars on the road.
Then 3 more cars come.
How many cars are there?

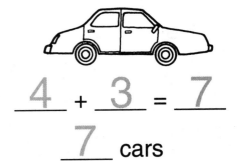

__4__ + __3__ = __7__

__7__ cars

2. Mr. Ladd sees 7 buses.
Then he sees 3 more buses.
How many buses does he see?

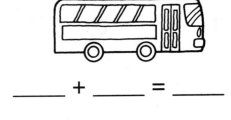

_____ + _____ = _____

_____ buses

3. Anna counts 3 stop signs.
Then she counts 6 more
stop signs. How many
stop signs does she see?

_____ + _____ = _____

_____ stop signs

4. Mr. Smith puts 4 new tires on
a truck and a car.
How many tires are there?

_____ + _____ = _____

_____ tires

Addition to 10: Word Problems

• • • • • • • • • • • • GOING AWAY • • • • • • • • • • • •

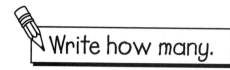
Write how many.

How many?	How many go away?	How many are left?

1.

_3_   _1_   _2_

2.

_____   _____   _____

3.

_____   _____   _____

Real World Connection

Look at the picture. Solve.

4. I see _____ ducks.

I see _____ walk away.

I see _____ left in the water.

Subtraction to 10: Concept Development of Subtraction

Name _____ Date _____

 Write the subtraction sentences and solve.

1. $\underline{4}$ – $\underline{2}$ = $\underline{2}$

2. ____ – ____ = ____

3. ____ – ____ = ____

4. ____ – ____ = ____

 Cross out. Then write how many are left.

5.

$4 - 2 =$ ____

6.

$6 - 1 =$ ____

Real World Connection

Write the subtraction sentence and solve.

7.

____ – ____ = ____ birds

Name _____ Date _____

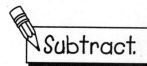 Subtract.

1.

$2 - 0 = \underline{\quad 2 \quad}$

2.

$3 - 3 = \underline{\qquad}$

3.

$6 - 6 = \underline{\qquad}$

4.

$4 - 0 = \underline{\qquad}$

5.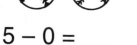

$5 - 0 = \underline{\qquad}$

6.

$4 - 4 = \underline{\qquad}$

Real World Connection

Write a subtraction sentence and solve.

7. There are 5 children.
There are 5 balls.
Each child gets a ball.
How many balls are left?

_____ – _____ = _____ balls

Subtraction to 10: Subtracting 0

Math 1, SV 8045-6

Name _____   Date _____

·············· **COOKIE COUNT** ··············

✎ Find ways to subtract from 5.

1. 5 − __5__ = __0__   **2.** 5 − _____ = _____

3. 5 − _____ = _____   **4.** 5 − _____ = _____

5. 5 − _____ = _____   **6.** 5 − _____ = _____

✎ Subtract.

7. 6 − 3 = _____   **8.** 6 − 2 = _____

9. 5 − 2 = _____   **10.** 5 − 1 = _____

11. 5 − 2 = _____   **12.** 5 − 3 = _____

13. 4 − 0 = _____   **14.** 4 − 1 = _____

Real World Connection

Write a subtraction sentence and solve.

15. Carlos puts 6 cookies in a bag.
He eats 3 cookies.
How many cookies are left?

_____ − _____ = _____ cookies

········ WHISTLE WHILE YOU WORK ········

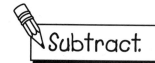

1.

$$\begin{array}{r} 4 \\ -\ 2 \\ \hline 2 \end{array}$$

2.

$$\begin{array}{r} 5 \\ -\ 1 \\ \hline \end{array}$$

3.

$$\begin{array}{r} 6 \\ -\ 0 \\ \hline \end{array}$$

4.

$$\begin{array}{r} 4 \\ -\ 3 \\ \hline \end{array}$$

5.

$$\begin{array}{r} 5 \\ -\ 5 \\ \hline \end{array}$$

6.

$$\begin{array}{r} 6 \\ -\ 1 \\ \hline \end{array}$$

7.

$$\begin{array}{r} 6 \\ -\ 4 \\ \hline \end{array}$$

8.

$$\begin{array}{r} 5 \\ -\ 4 \\ \hline \end{array}$$

Real World Connection

Write a subtraction sentence and solve.

9. Rosa has 4 whistles.
She gives 1 away.
How many whistles does she have left?

_____ − _____ = _____ whistles

HOPPING BACK

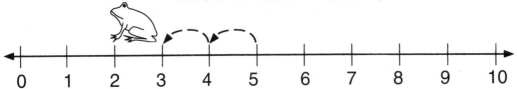

$$5 - 2 = \underline{}3\underline{}$$

Use the number line. Count back to subtract.

(4,3)

1. $4 - 1 = \underline{}3$

(3,2)

2. $3 - 1 = \underline{}$

3. $6 - 1 = \underline{}$

4. $5 - 2 = \underline{}$

5. $5 - 1 = \underline{}$

6. $7 - 2 = \underline{}$

7. $9 - 2 = \underline{}$

8. $3 - 2 = \underline{}$

9. $7 - 1 = \underline{}$

10. $9 - 1 = \underline{}$

11. $6 - 2 = \underline{}$

12. $8 - 1 = \underline{}$

13. $10 - 1 = \underline{}$

14. $10 - 2 = \underline{}$

Real World Connection

Write a subtraction sentence and solve.

15. 7 frogs sit on a log.
2 frogs hop off.
How many frogs are left?

_____ – _____ = _____ frogs

Subtraction to 10: Counting Back

Name _____   Date _____

$$9 \quad \boxed{9,8}$$
$$-1$$
$$\overline{8}$$

$$7 \quad \boxed{7,6,5}$$
$$-2$$
$$\overline{5}$$

$$6 \quad \boxed{6,5,4}$$
$$-2$$
$$\overline{4}$$

✏️ Count back to subtract.

1. $\begin{array}{r} 8 \\ -1 \\ \hline \end{array}$	**2.** $\begin{array}{r} 10 \\ -1 \\ \hline \end{array}$	**3.** $\begin{array}{r} 4 \\ -1 \\ \hline \end{array}$	**4.** $\begin{array}{r} 5 \\ -1 \\ \hline \end{array}$	**5.** $\begin{array}{r} 3 \\ -1 \\ \hline \end{array}$
6. $\begin{array}{r} 3 \\ -2 \\ \hline \end{array}$	**7.** $\begin{array}{r} 10 \\ -2 \\ \hline \end{array}$	**8.** $\begin{array}{r} 5 \\ -2 \\ \hline \end{array}$	**9.** $\begin{array}{r} 4 \\ -2 \\ \hline \end{array}$	**10.** $\begin{array}{r} 9 \\ -2 \\ \hline \end{array}$
11. $\begin{array}{r} 7 \\ -1 \\ \hline \end{array}$	**12.** $\begin{array}{r} 9 \\ -2 \\ \hline \end{array}$	**13.** $\begin{array}{r} 9 \\ -1 \\ \hline \end{array}$	**14.** $\begin{array}{r} 6 \\ -2 \\ \hline \end{array}$	**15.** $\begin{array}{r} 5 \\ -1 \\ \hline \end{array}$

Real World Connection

Write a subtraction sentence and solve.

16. A train has 10 cars.
2 cars are taken off.
How many cars are left?

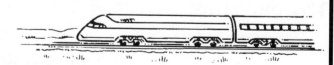

_____ – _____ = _____ cars

Subtraction to 10: Counting Back Using Mental Math

Math 1, SV 8045-6

Name _____ Date _____

Subtract.

1. 6
−1
5

2. 4
−0

3. 3
−3

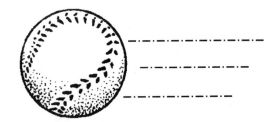
- - - - - - - - - -
- - - - - - - - - -
- - - - - - - - - -

4. 6
−2

5. 9
−7

6. 10
−1

7. 4
−3

8. 10
−7

9. 10
−2

10. 9
−8

11. 7
−2

12. 8
−5

13. 9
−6

14. 7
−3

15. 6
−4

16. 5
−3

17. 7
−1

18. 10
−9

Real World Connection

Write a subtraction sentence and solve.

19. Jack has 8 balls.
Fred has 3 balls.
How many more balls does Jack have?

_____ − _____ = _____ balls

Subtraction to 10: Subtraction Practice

38

Math 1, SV 8045-6

Name _____ Date _____

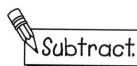

1.   6
        − 2
      _____

2.   8
        − 1
      _____

3.   9
        − 3
      _____

4. 10
        − 1
      _____

5.   5
        − 3
      _____

6.   9
        − 2
      _____

7.   7
        − 3
      _____

8.   8
        − 2
      _____

9.   9
        − 1
      _____

10. 10
        − 3
      _____

11. 7
        − 2
      _____

12. 6
        − 1
      _____

13. 10
        − 2
      _____

14. 8
        − 3
      _____

15. 7
        − 1
      _____

16. 4
        − 4
      _____

17. 8
        − 0
      _____

18. 6
        − 3
      _____

Real World Connection

Write a subtraction sentence and solve.

19. Tran had 10 balloons.
    He let 6 go.
    How many balloons did he have left?

_____ − _____ = _____ balloons

Subtraction to 10: Subtraction Practice

Math 1, SV 8045-6

Name _____ Date _____

 ············ **WATCH THE SIGN!** ············

┌─────────────────────┐
│ ✏ Add or subtract. │
└─────────────────────┘

1.

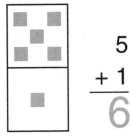
$$\begin{array}{r} 5 \\ + 1 \\ \hline 6 \end{array}$$

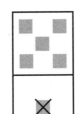
$$\begin{array}{r} 6 \\ - 1 \\ \hline \end{array}$$

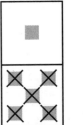
$$\begin{array}{r} 6 \\ - 5 \\ \hline \end{array}$$

2.

$$\begin{array}{r} 2 \\ + 4 \\ \hline \end{array}$$

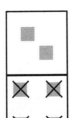
$$\begin{array}{r} 6 \\ - 4 \\ \hline \end{array}$$

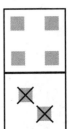
$$\begin{array}{r} 6 \\ - 2 \\ \hline \end{array}$$

3.

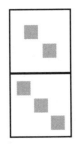
$$\begin{array}{r} 2 \\ + 3 \\ \hline \end{array}$$

$$\begin{array}{r} 5 \\ - 3 \\ \hline \end{array}$$

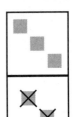
$$\begin{array}{r} 5 \\ - 2 \\ \hline \end{array}$$

┌──┐
│ **Real World Connection** │
│ │
│ **Write a number sentence and solve.** │
│ 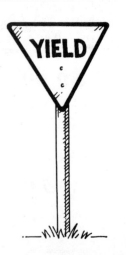 │
│ **4.** Inga saw 4 yield signs. │
│ She saw 7 stop signs. │
│ How many more stop signs did she see? │
│ │
│ ____ ⟵◯⟶ ____ = ____ stop signs │
└──┘

Name _____ Date _____

 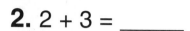 **FAST FACTS**

| Add or subtract. Write the numbers in each fact family. |

1. 5 + 1 = __6__

1 + 5 = __6__

6 − 1 = __5__

6 − 5 = __1__

__5__, __1__, __6__

2. 2 + 3 = _____

3 + 2 = _____

5 − 3 = _____

5 − 2 = _____

_____, _____, _____

 | Add or subtract. |

3.

2 + 6 = _____

6 + 2 = _____

8 − 2 = _____

8 − 6 = _____

4.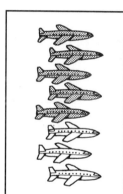

5 + 3 = _____

3 + 5 = _____

8 − 5 = _____

8 − 3 = _____

Real World Connection

Write a number sentence and solve.

5. Greg has these toy cars.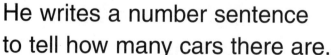
He writes a number sentence
to tell how many cars there are.
What number sentence can Greg write?

_____ ◯ _____ = _____ cars

Subtraction to 10: Fact Families

© Steck-Vaughn Company

Math 1, SV 8045-6

Name _____   Date _____

Add or subtract.

1.   2
     $+0$

2.   9
     -1

3.   3
     $+3$

4.   7
     -3

5.   6
     -2

6.   5
     $+4$

7.   7
     $+3$

8.   4
     $+4$

9.   2
     $+5$

10.   3
      $+4$

11.   7
      $+1$

12.   6
      -0

13.   8
      $+2$

14.   0
      $+0$

15.   10
      -6

16.   3
      -1

17.   4
      $+2$

18.   7
      -3

19.   9
      $+1$

20.   8
      -4

21.   5
      $+5$

22.   9
      -2

23.   6
      -6

Real World Connection

Write a number sentence and solve.

24. Sonya has these cats.
   She writes a number sentence
   to tell how many cats there are in all.
   What number sentence can Sonya write?

_____ ◯ _____ = _____ cats

Subtraction to 10: Mixed Practice

         Math 1, SV 8045-6

······· HIKING TO SOLVE PROBLEMS ·······

Write the number sentences and solve.

1. The Davis family takes a hike.

Mrs. Davis finds 2 .

Then she finds 5 more.

How many in all?

_____ ◯ _____ = _____

2. Mr. Davis see 6 .

Then 1 hops away.

How many are left?

_____ ◯ _____ = _____

3. Chad watches 4 .

Then 3 run away.

How many are left?

_____ ◯ _____ = _____

4. Rosa counts 7 .

Then she counts 3 more.

How many in all?

_____ ◯ _____ = _____

Subtraction to 10: Word Problems

Math 1, SV 8045-6

Name _____ Date _____

• • • • • • • • • • • A BUNCH OF CARROTS • • • • • • • • • • •

✎ Write how many groups. Write how many in all.

1.

___3___ groups of 10

___30___

2.

_____ groups of 10

_____

3.

_____ groups of 10

_____

Real World Connection

Solve.

4. Robert buys 40 carrots for his rabbit.
Circle how many carrots Robert buys.

Place Value: Grouping Tens

44   Math 1, SV 8045-6

·········· OODLES OF NOODLES ··········

 Show each number. Write how many.

1. ⊂⊂⊂⊂⊂⊂⊂⊂⊂⊂
⊂

___1___ ten ___1___ one

11

2. ⊂⊂⊂⊂⊂⊂⊂⊂⊂⊂
⊂ ⊂

____ ten ____ ones

____

3. ⊂⊂⊂⊂⊂⊂⊂⊂⊂⊂
⊂⊂⊂⊂⊂⊂

____ ten ____ ones

____

4. ⊂⊂⊂⊂⊂⊂⊂⊂⊂⊂
⊂⊂⊂⊂⊂⊂⊂⊂⊂⊂

____ tens ____ ones

____

Real World Connection

Solve.

5. The game has 20 white cubes.
It has 1 red cube.
How many cubes does the
game have in all?

_____ cubes

Place Value: Tens and Ones

Math 1, SV 8045-6

• • • • • • • • • • • • BUILDING BLOCKS • • • • • • • • • • • •

 Count. Write how many in all.

1. 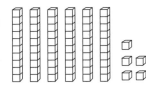 65

2. 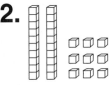 _____

3. 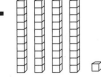 _____

4. 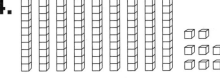 _____

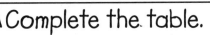 Complete the table.

	Tens	Ones	In All
5.	7	4	74
6.	8	0	_____
7.	9	6	_____

Real World Connection

Solve.

8. Deena can put 52 blocks in a box.
Circle the blocks Deena will put in the box.

Place Value: Tens and Ones with Models

Name _____ Date _____

 • • • • • • • • **COUNTING MAKES "CENTS"** • • • • • • • •

Count. Write how many pennies in all.

10 pennies

1.

12

2.

_____

3.

_____

4.

_____

Real World Connection

Solve.

5. Jose has 13¢.

Circle the group of pennies that Jose has.

Place Value: Counting Pennies

•••••••••• BOXES OF BLOCKS ••••••••••

Circle the number that is greater.

1. (55)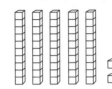

34

2. 46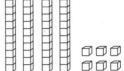

48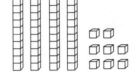

3. 28

82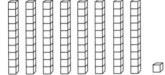

4. 69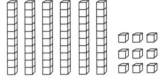

39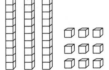

Real World Connection

Solve.

5. Gina has 59 blocks in a box.
Kim has 63 blocks in a box.
Who has more?
Circle the name.

Gina   Kim

Place Value: Comparing Numbers

Math 1, SV 8045-6

············· **LINES OF NUMBERS** ············

Write the numbers.

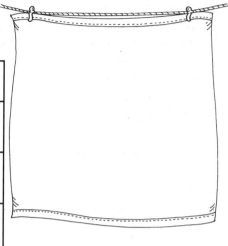

	before	between	after
1.	_21_	22	_23_
2.	_____	47	_____
3.	_____	97	_____

 Write the number that comes between.

4.	37 _38_ 39	12 _____ 14	20 _____ 22
5.	91 _____ 93	25 _____ 27	78 _____ 80
6.	22 _____ 24	86 _____ 88	32 _____ 34

Real World Connection

Solve.

7. Mr. Evans washed the team shirts.
What shirt is missing a number?
Write the number.

Place Value: Number Order

Math 1, SV 8045-6

Name _____   Date _____

 Write the missing numbers.

1. 61 ___ ___ ___ 65 ___ 67 ___ ___ ___

2. 56 57 ___ ___ ___ 61 ___ ___ ___ ___

3. ___ ___ 23 24 ___ ___ ___ ___ ___ 30

4. 45 46 ___ ___ ___ 50 ___ ___ ___ 54

5. 89 ___ ___ 92 ___ ___ 95 ___ 97 ___

Real World Connection

Solve.

6. Keesha is missing some pieces of her puzzle. Write the numbers in order to show which numbers are missing.

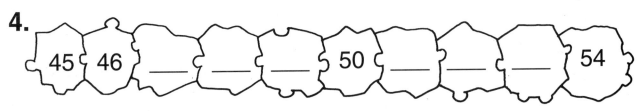

___ ___ ___ ___ ___ ___ ___

Place Value: Number Order

Math 1, SV 8045-6

•••• CHECKING OUT PROBLEM SOLVING ••••

 Solve.

1. The library checked out these books in one day. Write how many.

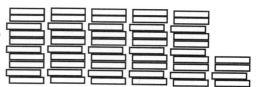

_____ books

2. There are 10 books on each shelf.
There are 7 shelves.
Write how many books.

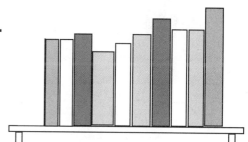

_____ books

3. Sally checks out a book with 32 pages.
Sam checks out a book with 23 pages.
Who has more pages to read?
Circle the name.

Sally   Sam

4. Lisa finds a book that is missing some pages.
Write the missing page numbers.

| 45 | ___ | ___ | 48 | 49 | ___ | 51 |

51

Place Value: Word Problems
Math 1, SV 8045-6

•••••••••• NUTS ABOUT ADDING ••••••••••

Do these in your head. Then write the sums.

1. 1 + 1 = 2, so 1 + 2 = __3__.

2. 4 + 4 = 8, so 4 + 5 = _____.

3. 0 + 0 = 0, so 0 + 1 = _____.

4. 8 + 8 = _____ , so 8 + 9 = _____.

5. 7 + 7 = _____ , so 7 + 8 = _____.

Look for doubles to find the sums.

6.	**7.**	**8.**	**9.**	**10.**
5	3	6	4	3
+ 5	+ 3	+ 7	+ 5	+ 4

11.	**12.**	**13.**	**14.**	**15.**
8	5	8	4	6
+ 8	+ 6	+ 9	+ 4	+ 6

Real World Connection

Write an addition sentence and solve.

16. A mother squirrel eats 6 nuts.
Another squirrel eats 5 nuts.
How many nuts do they eat in all?

_____ + _____ = _____ nuts

Addition and Subtraction to 18: Doubles and Doubles Plus 1

Math 1, SV 8045-6

Name _____ Date _____

"SUM" FRAMING

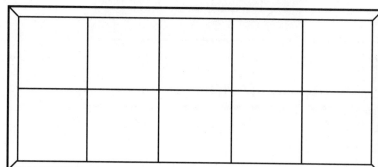

Use counters and the 10-frame.
Start with the greater number. Make a 10. Then add.

1. 7
+ 4
11

2. 8
+ 6

3. 3
+ 9

4. 4
+ 8

5. 5
+ 9

6. 9
+ 6

7. 3
+ 8

8. 7
+ 5

9. 2
+ 9

10. 5
+ 8

11. 6
+ 8

12. 4
+ 9

13. 7
+ 9

14. 4
+ 7

15. 8
+ 3

Real World Connection

Write an addition sentence and solve.

16. Chan hangs 9 pictures on a wall.
He hangs 4 more on the wall.
How many pictures does he have in all?

_____ + _____ = _____ pictures

Addition and Subtraction to 18: Make a Ten

· · · · "SUM" DIFFERENCES ABOUT BOOKS · · · ·

Write the addition facts that help.
Then complete the subtraction facts.

STORY
BOOK

1. 12
   − 5
   ___
   7 | 7
      | + 5
      | ___
      | 12

2. 14
   − 5
   ___

3. 12
   − 3
   ___

4. 13
   − 8
   ___

5. 11
   − 4
   ___

6. 12
   − 8
   ___

7. 14
   − 7
   ___

8. 13
   − 6
   ___

9. 11
   − 9
   ___

10. 12
   − 6
   ___

11. 14
   − 8
   ___

Real World Connection

Write a number sentence and solve.

12. Jane read 4 books.
   Her mother read 8 books.
   How many books in all did they read?

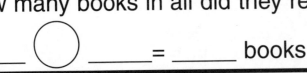

_____ ◯ _____ = _____ books

Addition and Subtraction to 18: Facts to 14

Name _____ Date _____

CLEAR AS GLASS

Write the sum and difference for each pair.

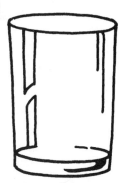

1.   4   12
    + 8   − 8

2.   8   16
    + 8   − 8

3.   9   17
    + 8   − 8

4.   7   15
    + 8   − 8

5.   7   16
    + 9   − 9

6.   7   14
    + 7   − 7

7.   6   15
    + 9   − 9

8.   9   18
    + 9   − 9

Real World Connection

Write a number sentence and solve.

9. Molly washed 16 glasses.
Her brother washed 9 glasses.
How many more glasses did Molly wash?

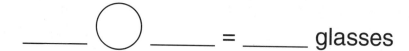

_____ ◯ _____ = _____ glasses

Addition and Subtraction to 18: Facts to 18

Math 1, SV 8045-6

Name _____ Date _____

 | Write each fact family. |

1.  $\underline{6} + \underline{7} = \underline{13}$ | $\underline{7} + \underline{6} = \underline{13}$
$\underline{13} - \underline{7} = \underline{6}$ | $\underline{13} - \underline{6} = \underline{7}$

6 7
13

2. 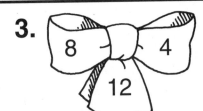   ___ + ___ = ___ | ___ + ___ = ___
___ − ___ = ___ | ___ − ___ = ___

6 9
15

3.    ___ + ___ = ___ | ___ + ___ = ___
___ − ___ = ___ | ___ − ___ = ___

8 4
12

4.   ___ + ___ = ___ | ___ + ___ = ___
___ − ___ = ___ | ___ − ___ = ___

6 5
11

Real World Connection

Solve.

5. Meg makes 8 red bows and 6 blue bows.
She writes a number sentence to tell
how many bows there are.
What number sentence can Meg write?

_____

Addition and Subtraction to 18: Fact Families

Name _____ Date _____

• • • • • • • • • • COLORING PRACTICE • • • • • • • • • • •

Add or subtract to solve.

1.   8
   + 5
_____

2. 12
  − 7
_____

3.   6
  + 6
_____

4. 11
  − 4
_____

5.   4
  + 9
_____

6.   7
  + 7
_____

7. 16
  − 9
_____

8. 14
  − 7
_____

9. 12
  − 7
_____

10.   9
   + 2
_____

11. 13
   − 7
_____

12.   9
   + 9
_____

13. 17
   − 8
_____

14. 16
   − 7
_____

15. 14
   − 8
_____

16.   8
   + 3
_____

17. 11
   − 6
_____

18.   8
   + 7
_____

19.   9
   + 5
_____

20.   8
   + 8
_____

21. 15
   − 9
_____

22.   6
   + 7
_____

23.   9
   + 8
_____

Real World Connection

Write a number sentence and solve.

24. Chad has 16 crayons.
He gives 8 crayons to a friend.
How many crayons does he have left?

_____ ◯ _____ = _____ crayons

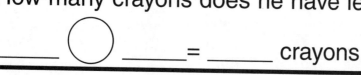

Addition and Subtraction to 18: Mixed Practice

Math 1, SV 8045-6

Name _____ Date _____

····· PROBLEM SOLVING WITH PUPPIES ·····

Solve.

1. There are 14 puppy treats in a box.
Spot eats 5 treats.
How many treats are left?

_____ ◯ _____ = _____ treats

2. There are 6 black puppies at the pet store.
There are 7 brown puppies, too.
How many puppies are there in all?

_____ ◯ _____ = _____ puppies

3. Jack has 3 dogs.
One dog had 8 puppies.
How many dogs does Jack have in all?

_____ ◯ _____ = _____ dogs

4. Ling's puppy is 17 weeks old.
She got it when it was 8 weeks old.
How many weeks has Ling had her puppy?

_____ ◯ _____ = _____ weeks

Addition and Subtraction to 18: Word Problems

Math 1, SV 8045-6

Name _____ Date _____

 Circle each shape that will stack.

1.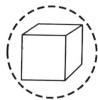

Draw an X on each shape that will roll.

2.

Color each shape that will slide.

3.

Real World Connection

Solve.

4. Ed uses these solid shapes to build.
Circle the shape he must put on top.
Tell why.

_____

_ _

_____

• • • • • • • • CAN YOU FIGURE IT OUT? • • • • • • • •

Match the plane shape to the solid.

1. •   •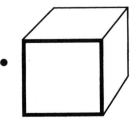

2.  •   •

3. •   •

4. 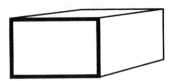 •   •

Real World Connection

Solve.

5. Kwan has a block that has 1 square side
   and 4 triangle sides.
   Circle the block he has.

Geometry: Solid and Plane Shapes

Name _____   Date _____

• • • • • • • • AN OPEN AND SHUT CASE • • • • • • • •

| Color inside each closed figure. |
| Circle the figures that are open. |

open   closed

1.

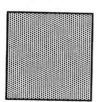   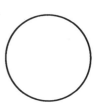

2.

 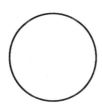  

| Color inside each rectangle. |

3.

  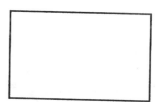 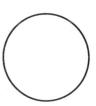

Real World Connection

Solve.

4. Circle the letters that are open figures.

C D G N O S

Geometry: Open and Closed Figures

Math 1, SV 8045-6

Name _____   Date _____

 Write how many sides and corners.

1.

corner

side

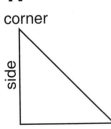

__3__ sides

__3__ corners

2.

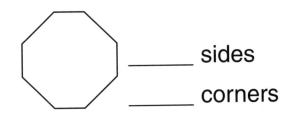

_____ sides

_____ corners

3.

_____ sides

_____ corners

4.

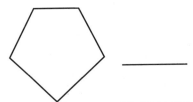

_____ sides

_____ corners

5.

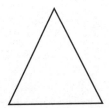

_____ sides

_____ corners

6.

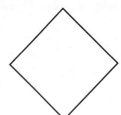

_____ sides

_____ corners

Real World Connection

Solve.

7. Katie drew a figure that has 2 sides and 1 corner.
What figure did she draw? Circle the answer.

open figure   closed figure

Geometry: Sides and Corners

Math 1, SV 8045-6

Name _____ Date _____

• • • • • • • • RIGHT DOWN THE MIDDLE • • • • • • • •

Draw a line to make two parts that match.

1.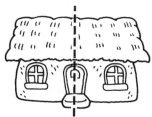

2.

3.

4.

5.

6.

7.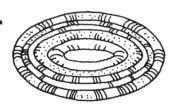

8.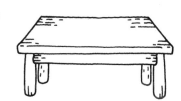

Real World Connection

Solve.

9. Linda has these sheets of paper.
Which can she fold so they are the same?
Circle the shapes.

Geometry: Symmetry

Math 1, SV 8045-6

Name _____   Date _____

 Circle the ones that are the same shape and size.

1.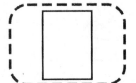

2.

3.

4.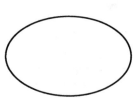

Real World Connection

Solve.

5. David makes this shape on one side of his paper.
He wants to make the same shape on the other side.
Draw the shape David will make.

Name _____   Date _____

GOING IN CIRCLES

Color the circles to continue the pattern.
Color R circles ▭ red ▷ . Color B circles ▭ blue ▷ .

1.

(R) (B) (B) (R) (B) (B) (R) (B) (B) ( )

2.

(R) (B) (R) (B) (R) (B) (R) (B) (R) ( )

3.

(R) (R) (B) (B) (R) (R) (B) (B) (R) ( )

Real World Connection

Solve.

4. Holly writes these numbers.
Write a number to continue the pattern.

4 1 2 4 1 2 4 1 2 4 _____

Geometry: Patterns

Math 1, SV 8045-6

Name _____   Date _____

··· PROBLEM SOLVING THE "WRITE" WAY ···

Solve.

1. Ned writes a letter on his paper.
   It is an open figure.
   It has 4 sides.
   It is a letter between T and X.
   What letter does Ted write? _____

2. Elena writes with a piece of chalk.
   What shape is the chalk?
   Circle the answer.

   cylinder   cone

3. Anna writes a letter that has
   no sides and no corners.
   It is a closed letter.
   It is between M and P.
   What letter does Anna write? _____

4. Manny traces the bottom of this box.
   What shape will he see on the paper?
   Circle the answer.

   triangle   square

Geometry: Word Problems

······· MEASURING AT A STEADY CLIP ······

Find these objects in your classroom.
About how many 🖇 long is each one?
Estimate. Then use 🖇 to measure.

Objects	Estimate	Measurement
1.	about _____ 🖇	about _____ 🖇
2.	about _____ 🖇	about _____ 🖇
3.	about _____ 🖇	about _____ 🖇
4.	about _____ 🖇	about _____ 🖇

Real World Connection

Solve.

5. Rita has a ✏️ . Max has a 🖇 .
Who would use more lengths to measure a desk?
Circle the name. Tell why.

Rita   Max

_____

- -

_____

Measurement: Using Nonstandard Units

Math 1, SV 8045-6

Name _____   Date _____

• • • • • • • • • • • • • INCH BY INCH • • • • • • • • • • • • •

Use your inch ruler to measure. Write how many inches tall.

1.

5 | 4 | 3 | 2 | 1 | inches

_5_ inches

2.

_____ inches

4.

_____ inches

3.

_____ inches

Real World Connection

Solve.

5. Holly finds a pine needle 4 inches long.
Draw a pine needle to show how long.

Measurement: Inches

Name _____   Date _____

········ MEASUREMENT WITH CLASS ········

Find these objects in your classroom.
About how many centimeters long is each one?
Estimate. Then use a centimeter ruler to measure.

	Objects	Estimate	Measurement
1.	chalk	about _____ centimeters	about _____ centimeters
2.	desk	about _____ centimeters	about _____ centimeters
3.	book	about _____ centimeters	about _____ centimeters

Real World Connection

Solve.

4. Tim measures this paper from top to bottom.
He says it measures 11.
Circle the kind of measurement he used.

inch   centimeter

Name _____ Date _____

"WEIGHT" AND SEE

Circle the object in each pair that is heavier.

1.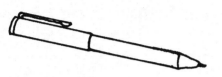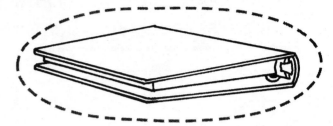

2.

3.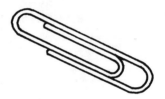

4.

Real World Connection

Solve.

5. Anita puts these objects on a balance.
Circle the heaviest object.

cup   pan   block

Measurement: Estimating Weight

Math 1, SV 8045-6

•••••••••••••• **ALL FILLED UP!** ••••••••••••••

 Circle the better estimate.

1.

more than 1 quart

less than 1 quart

2.

more than 1 cup

less than 1 cup

 Color the cups to show the same amount.

3.

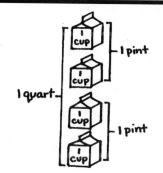

Pint

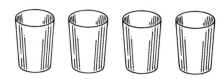

4.

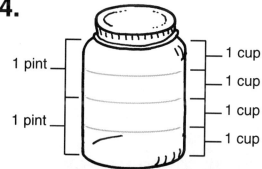

Quart

Real World Connection

Solve.

5. Marta has 1 quart of juice.
How many cups can she fill?

_____ cups

Measurement: Capacity

Math 1, SV 8045-6

Name _____   Date _____

 •••••••••••• **SOME LIKE IT HOT!** •••••••••••

Circle the one in each pair that is hot.

1.

2.

3.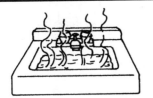

4.

Real World Connection

Solve

5. Ellen measures the temperature of these objects.
Circle the one that shows the hottest temperature.

Measurement: Estimating Temperature

Name _____   Date _____

 Solve.

1. Mark has a pencil box that is 8 inches long.
His pencil is 7 inches long.
Will his pencil fit in the box?
Circle <u>yes</u> or <u>no</u>.

yes   no

2. Fran wants the biggest jar
of paint she can buy.
Circle the paint Fran will buy.

3. Mark has a crayon that is 7 centimeters long.
Use a ruler. Draw a crayon 7 centimeters long.

4. Isa left her crayons outside.
Her crayons melted.
What was the temperature?
Circle the picture to show what the temperature was.

      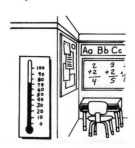

Measurement: Word Problems

Name _____ Date _____

 Circle the ones that show equal shares.

1.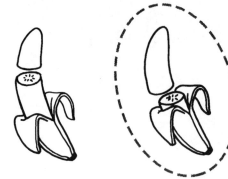

2.

3.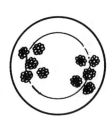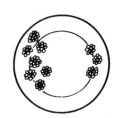

4.

5.

6.

Real World Connection

Solve.

7. Jim and Rhonda want
equal shares of pizza.
How should the pizza be cut?
Draw a line to show equal parts.

Fractions: Equal Parts

         Math 1, SV 8045-6

·········· NUTS ABOUT HALVES ··········

Draw a line to show two equal parts.
Then color to show $\frac{1}{2}$.

1.
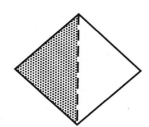

2.

3.
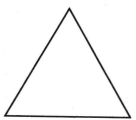

4.
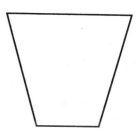

Find the shapes that show two equal parts. Color $\frac{1}{2}$.

5.
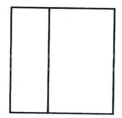 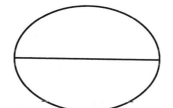 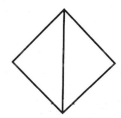

Real World Connection

Solve.

6. Two squirrels shared 4 nuts.
Each had one half of the 4 nuts.
How many nuts did each squirrel have?

_____ nuts

··········· FOLDED FRACTIONS ···········

 Circle the fraction that each shape shows.

1.

$\frac{1}{2}$ $\frac{1}{3}$

2.

$\frac{1}{2}$ $\frac{1}{3}$

3.

$\frac{1}{2}$ $\frac{1}{3}$

4.

$\frac{1}{2}$ $\frac{1}{3}$

5.

$\frac{1}{2}$ $\frac{1}{3}$

Find the shapes that show three equal parts. Color $\frac{1}{3}$.

6.

7.

Real World Connection

Solve.

8. The teacher asks the class to fold their paper into thirds. Did Allen follow directions? Circle <u>yes</u> or <u>no</u>.

yes   no

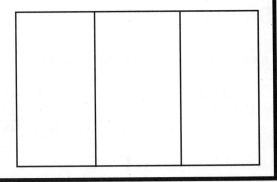

Fractions: Thirds

Math 1, SV 8045-6

Name _____   Date _____

 Circle the fraction that each shape shows.

1.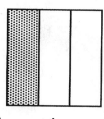

$\frac{1}{2}$ $\frac{1}{3}$ $\frac{1}{4}$

2.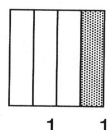

$\frac{1}{2}$ $\frac{1}{3}$ $\frac{1}{4}$

3.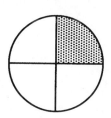

$\frac{1}{2}$ $\frac{1}{3}$ $\frac{1}{4}$

4.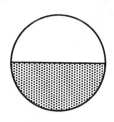

$\frac{1}{2}$ $\frac{1}{3}$ $\frac{1}{4}$

5.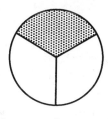

$\frac{1}{2}$ $\frac{1}{3}$ $\frac{1}{4}$

Find the shapes that show four equal parts. Color $\frac{1}{4}$.

6.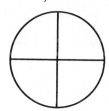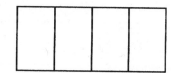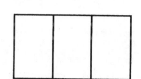

Real World Connection

Solve.

7. Sonya ate 1/2 of a pizza.
   Tim ate 1/4 of a pizza.
   Who ate more? Circle the name.   Sonya   Tim

Fractions: Fourths

77   Math 1, SV 8045-6

"BEARLY" A GROUP

 Color to show each fraction.

1.

$\frac{1}{2}$ blue

2.

$\frac{1}{4}$ red

3.

$\frac{1}{3}$ yellow

4.

$\frac{1}{2}$ purple, $\frac{1}{2}$ orange

5.

$\frac{1}{3}$ green, $\frac{1}{3}$ red, $\frac{1}{3}$ blue

Real World Connection

Solve.

6. There were 3 bears at the zoo. Kayla saw this bear. Write the fraction that tells what part of the group of the bears Kayla saw.

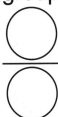

Fractions: Fractional Groups

Math 1, SV 8045-6

Name _____   Date _____

••• *PROBLEM SOLVING IS AS EASY AS PIE* ••••

 Solve.

1. Rob makes an apple pie.
He cuts all the apples in half.
Circle the way Rob cuts the apples.

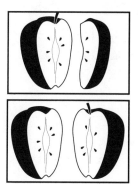

2. Claire ate a piece of pie.
What part of the pie did she eat?
Circle the answer.

$\frac{1}{2}$ $\frac{1}{3}$

3. Enrico cut a pie into 4 equal shares.
What part of the pie did he eat?
Circle the fraction.

$\frac{1}{4}$ $\frac{1}{3}$

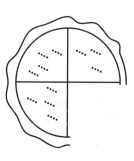

4. Pat gives $\frac{1}{3}$ of these pies to a friend.
Color the part of pies that she gives away.

Fractions: Word Problems

                                Math 1, SV 8045-6

Name _____ Date _____

• • • • • • • • • • • • SAY "WHEN"! • • • • • • • • • • • • •

Circle in green what happened first.
Circle in red what happened last.

1.

2.

3.
   Dear Grandma, How are you? I miss you. I have a new dog. He sleeps in my room.

Real World Connection

Solve.

4. Rob and Ann sell lemonade.
Write numbers to tell the order these events happen.

1 _____   _____   _____   _____

Time: Ordering Events

   Math 1, SV 8045-6

• • • • • • • • • • • • • • *HOW LONG?* **• • • • • • • • • •**

| Which takes more time to complete? Circle it. |

1.

2.

3.

Real World Connection

Solve.

4. Manny has these puzzles.
   Which takes the most time? Circle it.

Time: Estimating Time

                                       Math 1, SV 8045-6

•••••••••• READING TIME ••••••••••

 Trace the hour hand on each clock. Write the time.

1.

____3____ o'clock

2.

_____ o'clock

 Trace the minute hand on each clock.

3.

_____ o'clock

4.

_____ o'clock

5.

_____ o'clock

Real World Connection

Solve.

6. The clock shows 5 o'clock.
Clark reads for 1 hour.
Draw hands on the clock to show
the time now. Write the time.

_____ o'clock

Time: Reading an Analog Clock

Math 1, SV 8045-6

•••••••••••••••••• **CLOCKING IN** ••••••••••••••

Draw the hour hand so that both clocks show the same time.

1.

 1:00

2.

5:00

3.

11:00

 Write the time on the clock so that both clocks show the same time.

4.

5.

6.

Real World Connection

Solve.

7. Mr. Carlos gets to work at 8 o'clock. Write the time on the clock.

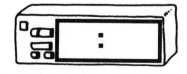

Time: Time to the Hour

Math 1, SV 8045-6

•••••••••••••• IT'S ON TIME ••••••••••••••

Circle the better estimate.

1.

Write your name 1 time.

more than 1 minute

less than 1 minute

2.

"This story is about . . ."

Tell a long story.

more than 1 minute

less than 1 minute

3.

"99, 98, 97, . . ."

Count backward from 99 to 1.

more than 1 minute

less than 1 minute

Real World Connection

Solve.

4. Circle the better estimate.
How long are you in school?

more than 1 hour   less than 1 hour

Time: Estimating Minutes

• • • • • • • • • • • • • • • **SPLASH TIME** • • • • • • • • • • • • • •

| Write each time. |

1.

8:00

2.

| : |

3.

| : |

4.

| : |

5.

| : |

| Show the time. Draw the minute hand. |

6.

10:00

7.

10:30

8.

11:00

Real World Connection

Solve.

9. Ron gets in the pool at 10:30.
He gets out in 30 minutes.
What time does Ron get out?
Write the time on the clock.

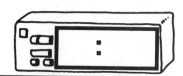

Time: Time to the Half Hour

Math 1, SV 8045-6

Name _____ Date _____

·········· CHECK YOUR CALENDAR ··········

Complete the calendar for next month.

_____, 19 _____

Sunday	Monday	Tuesday	Wednesday	Thursday	Friday	Saturday

Use the calendar. Write the answers.

1. How many days are in this month? _____ days

2. Name the first day of this month. _____

3. Name the last day of this month. _____

4. What day is today's date? _____

Real World Connection

Solve.

5. Look at the calendar for this year.
What day will your birthday fall on?

_____

Time: Calendar

PROBLEM SOLVING FROM START TO FINISH

 Solve.

1. Brenda started her picture at 3:00.
She finished 1 hour later.
Show the time she finished.

2. George started eating lunch at 12:00.
He finished 30 minutes later.
Show the time he finished.

3. The music started at 8:00.
It lasted 2 hours.
Show the time it ended.

Real World Connection

Solve.

4. Sue raked leaves. How long did she work?
Write the time.

_____ hours

Time: Word Problems

Math 1, SV 8045-6

FRUIT THAT MAKES CENTS

Circle how much money is needed.

1.

2.

3.

4.

Real World Connection

Solve.

5. Max has 2 nickels.
Can he buy the apple?
Circle <u>yes</u> or <u>no</u>.

yes   no

Name _____   Date _____

········· DIMES AND DINOSAURS ·········

Count by fives and tens. Circle how much money is needed.

1.

2.

3.

4.

5.

6.

Real World Connection

Solve.

7. Ellen has these coins.
Circle the greatest amount.

20 pennies   4 dimes   5 nickels

Money: Counting Dimes

Math 1, SV 8045-6

· · · · · · · · · · · · · **QUARTERBACK** · · · · · · · · · · · · ·

Write each amount.
Then circle the ones that have the same value as a .

1.

____20____ ¢

2.

_____ ¢

3.

_____ ¢

4.

_____ ¢

5.

_____ ¢

Real World Connection

Solve.

6. Nancy has 3 quarters. Can she buy a
football that costs 80¢? Circle <u>yes</u> or <u>no</u>.

yes   no

Money: Counting Quarters

Math 1, SV 8045-6

Name _____ Date _____

Count on. Write the amount.

1.

__10__ ¢ __20__ ¢ __30__ ¢ __31__ ¢ __32__ ¢ $\boxed{32}$ ¢

2.

____ ¢ ____ ¢ ____ ¢ ____ ¢ ____ ¢ $\boxed{}$ ¢

Write the amount.

3.

____ ¢

4.

____ ¢

Real World Connection

Solve.

5. Sue wants to buy a toy bear.
What coins will she need to buy it?

_____

Money: Counting Coins

Math 1, SV 8045-6

Name _____   Date _____

•••••••••••• COOL COUNTING ••••••••••••

 Count on. Write the amount.

1.

<u>25</u> ¢ <u>30</u> ¢ <u>31</u> ¢ <u>32</u> ¢ | 32 |¢

2.

____ ¢ ____ ¢ ____ ¢ ____ ¢ | |¢

3.

____ ¢ ____ ¢ ____ ¢ ____ ¢ ____ ¢ | |¢

4.

____ ¢ ____ ¢ ____ ¢ ____ ¢ ____ ¢ ____ ¢ | |¢

Real World Connection

Solve.

5. An ice cream costs 39¢.
Ryan has a quarter and a dime.
What coins will he need to buy it?

_____

Money: Counting Coins

© Steck-Vaughn Company   92   Math 1, SV 8045-6

········ THE SAME BUT DIFFERENT ········

Show a different way to make the same amount.
Draw the coins you used. Write the value on each coin.

1.

2.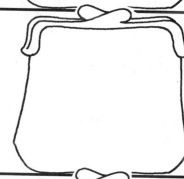

3.

Real World Connection

Solve.

4. Jessie has 2 dimes and 1 nickel.
Jack has 1 quarter and 3 pennies.
Who has more? Circle the name.

Jessie   Jack

Money: Equal Coin Amounts

Math 1, SV 8045-6

PROBLEM SOLVING CHANGES EVERYTHING

Solve.

1. Circle the amount that can be shown with the least amount of coins.

15¢   20¢   25¢

2. Sam has 2 dimes and 3 pennies.
Hal has 1 dime and 3 nickels.
Who has more? Ring the name.

Sam   Hal

3. Robert has 2 nickels and 4 dimes.
He trades the 2 nickels for 1 dime.
How much money does Robert have?

4. Sharon wants to buy the baseball.
She has 1 quarter and 1 dime.
Can she buy the baseball?
Circle <u>yes</u> or <u>no</u>.

yes   no

33¢

Money: Word Problems
Math 1, SV 8045-6

FIRST GRADE MATH
Answer Key

p. 5 1. 2 2. 6 3. 7 4. 5 5. 13 6. 7 7. 12 8. 7 9. 11 10. 15 11. 9 12. 14 13. 8 14. 10 15. 9 16. 7 17. 14 18. 17 19. 5 20. 7 21. 14 22. 6 23. 16 24. 7 25. 4 26. 13

p. 6 1. $7 + 3 = 10$; 10 2. $10 - 2 = 8$; 8 3. 8:00 4. $7 - 4 = 3$; 3

p. 7 1. squirrels, rabbits, birds, and turtles 2. 2 3. 1 4. 3 5. Students circle first group of 3 squirrels.

p. 8 1. 5 2. 4 3. 5 4. 4 5. 3 6. 5 7. 2 8. 4 9. 3 10. Students circle first and last groups.

p. 9 1. 6; six 2. 4; four 3. 0; zero 4. 5, five 5. 7; seven 6. 3; three 7. Students circle six tigers.

p. 10 1. Check students' work. 2. Check students' work. 3. 9

p. 11 1. nine; 9 2. seven; 7 3. ten; 10 4. eight; 8 5. 9

p. 12 1. 3 2. 0 3. 2 4. 0 5. 1 6. 4 7. Students circle bowl with 5 bananas.

p. 13 1. 5 2. 10 3. 7 4. 2 5. 4 6. 8, 7, 6, 3, 1 7. 9, 8, 5, 4, 3, 2 8. 7

p. 14 1. 6, 5; circle 6 2. 4, 9; circle 9 3. 5, 3; circle 3 4. 7, 9; circle 7 5. Lee

p. 15 1. 3 2. circle 4 pennies; write x on 3 pennies 3. 10 4. 8, 7, 5, 4, 3

p. 16 1. 4, 1, 5 2. 2, 1, 3 3. 5, 1, 6 4. 5

p. 17 1. $2 + 1 = 3$ 2. $4 + 1 = 5$ 3. $3 + 2 = 5$ 4. $5 + 1 = 6$ 5. $2 + 2 = 4$ 6. $2 + 2 = 4$

p. 18 1. 4; 4 2. 6; 6 3. 5; 5 4. Students circle first and second cubes.

p. 19 1. 2 2. 5 3. 1 4. 3 5. 4 6. 6

p. 20 1.-4. Position of answers may vary. $1 + 2 = 3$; $2 + 1 = 3$; $0 + 3 = 3$; $3 + 0 = 3$ 5.-9. Position of answers may vary. $1 + 3 = 4$; $3 + 1 = 4$; $0 + 4 = 4$; $4 + 0 = 4$; $2 + 2 = 4$ 10.-15. Position of answers may vary. $2 + 3 = 5$; $3 + 2 = 5$; $1 + 4 = 5$; $4 + 1 = 5$; $0 + 5 = 5$; $5 + 0 = 5$ 16. $3 + 2 = 5$ or $2 + 3 = 5$

p. 21 Check students' algorithms. 1. $1 + 3 = 4$ 2. $2 + 4 = 6$ 3. $3 + 2 = 5$ 4. $4 + 1 = 5$ or $1 + 4 = 5$

p. 22 1. 5 2. 6 3. 9 4. 7 5. 6 6. 4 7. 7 8. 9 9. 10 10. $6 + 2 = 8$

p. 23 1. circle 9; 10 2. circle 6; 8 3. circle 3; 5 4. circle 4; 6 5. circle 4; 7 6. circle 4; 5 7. circle 8; 10 8. circle 5; 8 9. circle 4; 5 10. circle 7; 10 11. $4 + 2 = 6$

p. 24 1. $4 + 4 = 8$ 2. $0 + 0 = 0$ 3. 6 4. 2 5. 4 6. 0 7. 10 8. 9 9. 8 10. 6; circle 11. 9 12. 10; circle 13. 8; circle 14. 10 15. 4; circle 16. 7 17. 2; circle 18. $3¢ + 3¢ = 6¢$

p. 25 1. 6; 7 2. 8; 9 3. 2 4. 5 5. 10 6. 6 7. 7 8. 5 9. 10 10. 8 11. 9 12. 10 13. $5 + 4 = 9$

p. 26 1. $6 + 4 = 10$ 2. $7 + 1 = 8$ 3. $2 + 6 = 8$ 4. 10 5. 8 6. 8 7. 10 8. 9 9. 9 10. 10 11. 9 12. 10 13. 10 14. $1 + 5 + 4 = 10$

p. 27 Check students' tables.; Peter and Jane

p. 28 1. 5 2. 7 3. 3 4. 4 5. 9 6. 9 7. 1 8. 9 9. 3 10. 10 11. 8 12. 8 13. 9 14. 9 15. 9 16. 10 17. 10 18. 8 19. 7 20. 6 21. 9 22. 7 23. 10 24. $3 + 5 = 8$

p. 29 1. 8 2. 9 3. 6 4. 10 5. 6 6. 10 7. 8 8. 7 9. 7 10. 10 11. 8 12. 4 13. 5 14. 0 15. 6 16. 7 17. 7 18. 10 19. 10 20. 8 21. 8 22. 8 23. 9 24. $2 + 3 = 5$

p. 30 1. $4 + 3 = 7$; 7 2. $7 + 3 = 10$; 10 3. $3 + 6 = 9$; 9 4. $4 + 4 = 8$; 8

p. 31 1. 3; 1 2. 2, 5; 1; 4 3. 2; 1; 1 4. 4; 2; 2

p. 32 1. $4 - 2 = 2$ 2. $5 - 2 = 3$ 3. $6 - 2 = 4$ 4. $3 - 1 = 2$ 5. 2 6. 5 7. $6 - 3 = 3$

p. 33 1. 2 2. 0 3. 0 4. 4 5. 5 6. 0 7. $5 - 5 = 0$

p. 34 1.-6. Answer order may vary. $5 - 5 = 0$; $5 - 4 = 1$; $5 - 3 = 2$; $5 - 2 = 3$; $5 - 1 = 4$; $5 - 0 = 5$ 7. 3 8. 4 9. 3 10. 4 11. 3 12. 2 13. 4 14. 3 15. $6 - 3 = 3$

p. 35 1. 2 2. 4 3. 6 4. 1 5. 0 6. 5 7. 2 8. 1 9. $4 - 1 = 3$

p. 36 1. 3 2. 2 3. 5 4. 3 5. 4 6. 5 7. 7 8. 1 9. 6 10. 8 11. 4 12. 7 13. 9 14. 8 15. $7 - 2 = 5$

p. 37 1. 7 2. 9 3. 3 4. 4 5. 2 6. 1 7. 8 8. 3 9. 2 10. 7 11. 6 12. 7 13. 8 14. 4 15. 4 16. $10 - 2 = 8$

p. 38 1. 5 2. 4 3. 0 4. 4 5. 2 6. 9 7. 1 8. 3 9. 8 10. 1 11. 5 12. 3 13. 3 14. 4 15. 2 16. 2 17. 6 18. 1 19. $8 - 3 = 5$

p. 39 1. 4 2. 7 3. 6 4. 9 5. 2 6. 7 7. 4 8. 6 9. 8 10. 7 11. 5 12. 5 13. 8 14. 5 15. 6 16. 0 17. 8 18. 3 19. $10 - 6 = 4$

p. 40 1. 6; 5; 1 2. 6; 2; 4 3. 5; 2; 3 4. $7 - 4 = 3$

p. 41 1. 6; 6; 5; 1; 5, 1, 6 2. 5; 5; 2; 3; 2, 3, 5 3. 8; 8; 6; 2; 2, 6, 8 4. 8; 8; 3; 5; 5, 3, 8 5. Answers will vary, but should include a number sentence with 6.

p. 42 1. 2 2. 8 3. 6 4. 4 5. 4 6. 9 7. 10 8. 8 9. 7 10. 7 11. 8 12. 6 13. 10 14. 0 15. 4 16. 2 17. 6 18. 4 19. 10 20. 4 21. 10 22. 7 23. 0 24. Answers will vary, but should include a number sentence with 1, 2, 3.

p. 43 1. $2 + 5 = 7$ 2. $6 - 1 = 5$ 3. $4 - 3 = 1$ 4. $7 + 3 = 10$

p. 44 1. 3; 30 2. 2; 20 3. 5; 50 4. Students circle 4 groups of 10.

p. 45 1. 1; 1; 11 2. 1; 2; 12 3. 1; 6; 16 4. 2; 0; 20 5. 21

p. 46 1. 65 2. 29 3. 41 4. 98 5. 74 6. 80 7. 96 8. Students should circle 5 rods and 2 cubes.

p. 47 1. 12 2. 35 3. 63 4. 44 5. Students circle last group of pennies.

p. 48 1. 55 2. 48 3. 82 4. 69 5. Kim

p. 49 1. 21; 23 2. 46; 48 3. 96; 98 4. 38; 13; 21 5. 92; 26; 79 6. 23; 87; 33 7. 70

p. 50 1. 62; 63; 64; 66; 68; 69; 70 2. 58; 59; 60; 62; 63; 64; 65 3. 21; 22; 25; 26; 27; 28; 29 4. 47; 48; 49; 51; 52; 53 5. 90; 91; 93; 94; 96; 98 6. 33; 35; 36

p. 51 1. 54 2. 70 3. Sally 4. 46; 47; 50

Math 1, SV 8045-6

p. 52 1. 3 2. 9 3. 1 4. 16; 17 5. 14; 15 6. 10 7. 6 8. 13 9. 9 10. 7 11. 16 12. 11 13. 17 14. 8 15. 12 16. 6 + 5 = 11

p. 53 1. 11 2. 14 3. 12 4. 12 5. 14 6. 15 7. 11 8. 12 9. 11 10. 13 11. 14 12. 13 13. 16 14. 11 15. 11 16. 9 + 4 = 13

p. 54 1. 7; 7 + 5 = 12 2. 9; 9 + 5 = 14 3. 9; 9 + 3 = 12 4. 5; 5 + 8 = 13 5. 7; 7 + 4 = 11 6. 4; 4 + 8 = 12 7. 7; 7 + 7 = 14 8. 7; 7 + 6 = 13 9. 2; 2 + 9 = 11 10. 6; 6 + 6 = 12 11. 6; 6 + 8 = 14 12. 4 + 8 = 12

p. 55 1. 12; 4 2. 16; 8 3. 17; 9 4. 15; 7 5. 16; 7 6. 14; 7 7. 15; 6 8. 18; 9 9. 16 − 9 = 7

p. 56 Answer order may vary. 1. 6 + 7 = 13; 7 + 6 = 13; 13 − 7 = 6; 13 − 6 = 7 2. 6 + 9 = 15; 9 + 6 = 15; 15 − 6 = 9; 15 − 9 = 6 3. 4 + 8 = 12; 8 + 4 = 12; 12 − 4 = 8; 12 − 8 = 4 4. 6 + 5 = 11; 5 + 6 = 11; 11− 5 = 6; 11 − 6 = 5 5. Answers will vary but should include a number sentence with 8, 6, 14.

p. 57 1. 13 2. 5 3. 12 4. 7 5. 13 6. 14 7. 7 8. 7 9. 5 10. 11 11. 6 12. 18 13. 9 14. 9 15. 6 16. 11 17. 5 18. 15 19. 14 20. 16 21. 6 22. 13 23. 17 24. 16 − 8 = 8

p. 58 1. 14 − 5 = 9 2. 6 + 7 = 13 3. 3 + 8 = 11 4. 17 − 8 = 9

p. 59 1. cube, cone, cylinder, cube 2. cone, cylinder, sphere 3. cone, cube, cylinder, cube 4. cone; No shapes can be stacked on the point of the cone.

p. 60 1. line from rectangle to rectangular prism 2. line from triangle to pyramid 3. line from circle to cylinder 4. line from square to cube 5. Students circle the pyramid.

p. 61 1. Students circle second and third figures and color first and fourth figures. 2. Students circle first and fourth figures and color second and third figures. 3. Students color first and third figures. 4. Students circle C, G, N, S.

p. 62 1. 3; 3 2. 8; 8 3. 4; 4 4. 5; 5 5. 3; 3 6. 4; 4 7. open figure

p. 63 1.-8. Check students' work to see that the pictures are symmetrical. 9. Students circle second and third figures.

p. 64 1. Students circle first, second, third figures. 2. Students circle first, fourth, fifth figures. 3. Students circle first, third, fifth figures. 4. Students circle first, second, third figures. 5. Check students' work for congruency.

p. 65 1. red 2. blue 3. red 4. 1

p. 66 1. W 2. cylinder 3. O 4. square

p. 67 1.-4. Answers will vary. 5. Max; pencils are longer than clips.

p. 68 1. 5 2. 2 3. 4 4. 1 5. Check students' drawings.

p. 69 1.-3. Answers will vary. 4. inch

p. 70 1. book 2. book 3. paste 4. crayons 5. pan

p. 71 1. less than 1 quart 2. more than 1 quart 3. Children color 2 glasses. 4. Children color 4 glasses. 5. 4

p. 72 1. teapot 2. hamburger 3. sink 4. boiling water 5. soup

p. 73 1. yes 2. second jar 3. Check students' work. 4. soup

p. 74 1.-6. Check students' work to see that they circled the equal parts. 7. Check students' work to see that the pizza shows equal parts.

p. 75 1.-4. Check students' work to see that they show 1/2. 5. Students color 1/2 of second and third figures. 6. 2

p. 76 1. 1/3 2. 1/2 3. 1/2 4. 1/3 5. 1/3 6. Students color second, third figures. 7. Students color third figure. 8. yes

p. 77 1. 1/3 2. 1/4 3. 1/4 4. 1/2 5. 1/3 6. Students color first, second figures. 7. Sonya

p. 78 1.-5. Check students' work. 6. 1/3

p. 79 1. Students circle apple cut in half. 2. 1/3 3. 1/4 4. Students color 1 pie.

p. 80 1. green-second cup; red-last cup 2. green-first pencil; red-third pencil 3. green-blank paper; red finished letter 4. 1, 4, 3, 2

p. 81 1. Students circle second picture. 2. Students circle first picture. 3. Students circle second picture. 4. Students circle second picture.

p. 82 1. 3 2. 7 3. 8 4. 5 5. 9 6. Children draw hands to show 6:00.; 6

p. 83 1.-3. Check students' work. 4. 6:00 5. 4:00 6. 2:00 7. 8:00

p. 84 1. less than 1 minute 2. more than 1 minute 3. more than 1 minute 4. more than 1 hour

p. 85 1. 8:00 2. 12:30 3. 2:30 4. 9:00 5. 5:00 6.-8. Check students' work. 9. 11:00

p. 86 1.-5. Check students' work.

p. 87 1. 4:00 2. 12:30 3. 10:00 4. 2

p. 88 1. Students circle 7 pennies. 2. Students circle 9 pennies. 3. Students circle 1 nickel. 4. Students circle 5 nickels. 5. yes

p. 89 1. Students circle 2 dimes. 2. Students circle 4 dimes. 3. Students circle 6 dimes. 4. Students circle 6 nickels. 5. Students circle 5 dimes. 6. Students circle 2 nickels. 7. 4 dimes

p. 90 1. 20 2. 40 3. 25; circle 4. 25; circle 5. 70 6. no

p. 91 1. 10, 20, 30, 31, 32; 32 2. 5, 10, 11, 12, 13; 13 3. 55 4. 27 5. Answers will vary.

p. 92 1. 25, 30, 31, 32; 32 2. 25, 35, 45, 50; 50 3. 25, 35, 40, 45, 46; 46 4. 25, 35, 45, 50, 55, 56; 56 5. 4 pennies

p. 93 1.-3. Answers will vary. 4. Jack

p. 94 1. 25¢ 2. Hal 3. 50¢ 4. yes